Handy Alaska Genealogy Handbook

I0423530

Gary L. Morris

Table of Contents

Obituaries

Wills and Probates

Immigration and Naturalization records

City Directories

Railroad records

Aleutian island Resources

Genealogical Research in Alaska

Alaska is the largest state in the United States, admitted to the union in 1959 as the 49th state. The land was acquired in 1867 from Russia when U.S. Secretary of State William Seward negotiated its purchase. Alaska was dubbed "Seward's Folly", as many believed the area to be worthless. When Gold was discovered in the 1890's a hoard of settlers and prospectors flocked the region, and of course genealogical records were created for them. On this page we will introduce you to those records, and help you to understand:

1. What they are

2. Where to find them

3. How to use them

These records can be found both online and off, so we'll introduce you to online websites, indexes and databases, as well as brick-and-mortar repositories and other institutions that will help with your research in Alaska. So that you will have a more comprehensive understanding of these records, we have provided a brief history of the "Land of the Midnight Sun" to illustrate what type of records may have been generated during specific time periods. That information will assist you in pinpointing times and locations on which to focus the search for your Alaska ancestors.

A Brief History of Alaska

It is believed Alaska was first inhabited by Siberian groups who crossed from Russia over what was known as the Bering land bridge, an extension of land that at one time connected Asia with North America. The first European settlers arrived in 1741; a group of Russian explorers led by one Vitus Bering, a Danish adventurer who had discovered the Being Strait in 1728. The Russians established the first settlement on Kodiak Island in 1784, and in 1867 Alaska was sold to the United States of America.

The agreement to purchase Alaska from Russia was initiated and signed by U.S. Secretary of State William H. Seward. At the time Alaska was thought to be a useless, barren land, but when oil and gold were discovered in the late 19th century, Alaska flourished and a genuine "colonial economy" developed. Alaska received territorial status in 1912, and entered statehood in 1959. When more oil was discovered at Prudhoe Bay in 1968, the concept of the Alaska Pipeline was born, a project that was completed in 1977 that sealed Alaska's economic value. The battle to balance the philosophies of conservation and development continue to this day.

Important Genealogical Dates in Alaska History

- **1741** - Discovered by Vitus Bering.

- **1783** - First European settlement established on Kodiak Island.

- **1799** – City of Sitka founded by the Russians and made capital of Alaska.

- **1824-1828** Alaska's boundaries established as latitude 54° 40 N and longitude 141° W

- **1867** - Alaska purchased from Russia by the United States.

- **1880** - First Federal Census enumerated.

- **1884** - Federal courts established.

- **1900** - Capital moved to Juneau.

- **1896** - Klondike Gold Rush brings more than 50,000 miners and other settlers to Alaska.

- **1912** - Alaska made a territory.

- **1959** - Alaska becomes 49th State.

Common Alaska Genealogical Issues and Resources to Overcome Them

Boundary Changes: A common obstacle when researching Alaska ancestors are historical boundary changes. One can be searching for an ancestor's record in one county when in fact it is stored in a different one due to historical county boundary changes. The **Atlas of Historical County Boundaries** can help you to overcome that problem. It provides a chronological listing of every boundary change that has occurred in the history of Alaska.

Atlas of Historical County Boundaries
http://publications.newberry.org/ahcbp/documents/AK_Consolidated_Chronology.htm#Consolidated_Chronology

Name Changes: Surname changes, variations, and misspellings can complicate genealogical research. It is important to check all spelling variations. Soundex, a program that indexes names by sound, is a useful first step, but you can't rely on it completely as some name variations result in different Soundex codes. The surnames could be different, but the first name may be different too. You can also find records filed under initials, middle names, and nicknames as well, so you will need to get creative with surname variations and spellings in order to cover all the possibilities.

You can find a Soundex Tutorial on the Family Search website: https://familysearch.org/learn/wiki/en/Soundex

Alaska Genealogical Archives and Libraries

Genealogical resources include not only records, but the organizations that house them, or can direct you to them. These institutions include: *Archives, Libraries, Genealogical Societies, Family History Centers, Universities, Churches, and Museums.*

Following are links to their websites, their physical addresses, and a summary of the records you can find there.

Archives

Alaska State Archives – The Alaska State Archives holds many records that are useful to genealogists such as; Naturalization records, Teacher records, Vital statistics, Probate records, World War I veterans records, and the Pioneer Home Residents index.

Alaska State Archives

PO Box 110525
141 Willoughby Avenue
Juneau, AK 99811-0525
Tel: 907.465.2270
Fax: 907.465.2465

Email: archives@alaska.gov

Website: http://archives.alaska.gov/genealogy/genealogy.html

National Archives at Anchorage, AK – Alaska census records, State Trooper records, and civil/criminal case records post 1959.

654 West Third Avenue,

Anchorage, AK 99501-2145

Tel: 907-261-7820
Fax: 907-261-7813

Email: alaska.archives@nara.gov

Website: http://www.archives.gov/anchorage/

Alaska State Library – Historical collection (maps, manuscripts, newspapers, photographs, and personal collections) census and burial records.

Alaska State Library and Historical Collections

PO Box 110571
333 Willoughby Avenue, 8th floor
Juneau, AK 99811-0571
Tel: 907.465.2920
Fax: 907.465.2151
Email: asl@alaska.gov
Email: asl.historical@alaska.gov

Website: http://library.alaska.gov/forpublic.html#genealogy

University of Alaska Anchorage Library – Gold rush collections, historical records, war records, newspapers, journals, mining records.

University of Alaska Anchorage
3211 Providence Drive
Anchorage, Alaska 99508
Tel: (907) 786-1800

Website: http://consortiumlibrary.org/

University of Alaska Fairbanks Elmer E. Rasmuson Library - historic photographs, manuscripts, rare books, maps, oral histories, and printed materials pertaining to Alaska and the Polar regions spanning six centuries.

University of Alaska Fairbanks
P.O. Box 757500
Fairbanks, AK 99775

Tel: 907-474-7211
E-mail: admissions@uaf.edu

Website: http://library.uaf.edu/university-records

Alaska Genealogical and Historical Societies

Genealogical and historical societies have access to extensive catalogues of genealogical data. They are also able to offer expert guidance for genealogical researchers. Many members are professional genealogists who are most willing to share their expertise in finding ancestors.

Alaska Historical Society – historical records, books, and research material

Website: http://www.alaskahistoricalsociety.org/index.cfm

Sheldon Museum & Cultural Center – Local and state histories, school records, ship logs, historical newspaper, transportation and industry histories.

Website: http://www.sheldonmuseum.org/research.htm

Baranov Museum - collection of materials chronicling the history of the Kodiak and Aleutian Islands region including library and archival materials, including books, manuscripts, photographs, newspapers, oral histories, film, and maps

Website:
http://www.baranovmuseum.org/index.php?option=com_content&task=view&id=46&Itemid=43

Fairbanks Genealogical Society – historical collections, death index, marriage records, ledgers, school records

Website: http://fairbanksgenealogicalsociety.com/

Alaska Family History Centers

The Family History Centers run by the LDS Church offer free access to billions of genealogical records for free to the general public. They also provide classes on genealogy and one-on-one assistance to inexperienced family historians. Here you will find a **Complete Listing of Alaska Family History Centers**.

Complete Listing of Alaska Family History Centers:
https://familysearch.org/locations/centerlocator

Additional Alaska Genealogical Resources

Alaska Mailing Lists

Mailing lists are internet based facilities that use email to distribute a single message to all who subscribe to it. When information on a particular surname, new records, or any other important genealogy information related to the mailing list topic becomes available, the subscribers are alerted to it. Joining a mailing list is an excellent way to stay up to date on Alaska genealogy research topics. Rootsweb have an extensive listing of **Alaska Mailing Lists** on a variety of topics.

Alaska Mailing Lists :
http://lists.rootsweb.ancestry.com/index/usa/AK/misc.html

Alaska Message Boards

A message board is another internet based facility where people can post questions about a specific genealogy topic and have it answered by other genealogists. If you have questions about a surname, record type, or research topic, you can post your question and other researchers and genealogists will help you with the answer. The message boards at the **Alaska Genealogy Forum** are completely free to use.

Alaska Genealogy Forum : http://genforum.genealogy.com/ak/

Alaska Newspapers and Periodicals

Many genealogy periodicals and historical newspapers contain reprinted copies of family genealogies, transcripts of family Bible records, information about local records and archives, census indexes, church records, queries, land records, obituaries, court records, cemetery records, and wills. These **Alaska Periodicals and Newspapers** are worth adding to your genealogical arsenal.

Alaska Periodicals and Newspapers :
http://alaskansavvy.com/alaska-information/alaska-media-information/alaska-newspapers-and-periodicals

Historical Alaska Maps and Gazetteers

Maps are necessary to genealogical research. They help us to locate landmarks, towns, cities, parishes, states, provinces, waterways and roads and streets. They also help us to determine when and where boundary changes might have taken place, and give us a visualization of the area we're researching in. For locating place names, a gazetteer is the best possible resource for any genealogist. Gazetteers are also sometimes called "place name dictionaries", and can help you to locate the area in which you need to conduct research. Below are links to the maps and gazetteers for research in Alaska.

Peabody GNIS Service – Alaska:
http://peabody.research.yale.edu/cgi-bin/Query.GNIS?ST=Alaska&SU=1

Color Landform Atlas – Alaska :
http://fermi.jhuapl.edu/states/ak_0.html

1985 U.S. Atlas : http://www.livgenmi.com/1895/AK/

Alaska Hometown Locator : http://alaska.hometownlocator.com/

Alaska Genealogical Records

<u>Birth, Death, Marriage and Divorce Records</u> – Birth, death, and marriage records are the most basic, yet most important records attached to your ancestor. They are generally referred to as vital records as they record vital life events. The reason for their importance is that they not only place your ancestor in a specific place at a definite time, but potentially connect the individual to other relatives. Below is a list of repositories where you can find Alaska vital records

Alaska Division of Public Health – Information may be requested via downloadable PDF form.

Vital Statistics
5441 Commercial Blvd.
Juneau, AK 99801
(907) 465-3391
(907) 465-3618, fax
Anchorage: (907) 269-0991
Fairbanks: (907) 452-4863

Website:
http://dhss.alaska.gov/dph/VitalStats/Pages/birth/default.aspx

Census Reports

Census records are among the most important genealogical documents for placing your ancestor in a particular place at a specific time. Like BDM records, they can also lead you to other ancestors, particularly those who were living under the authority of the head of household. Official Alaska census records exist from 1900-1930, but there are fragmented earlier reports dating from 1790 available. Following are the best places to find Alaska census records.

U.S National Archives – Alaska census records from 1790-1940

Website :
http://www.archives.gov/research/census/nonpopulation/alaska.html

Alaska State Library

Alaska State Library & Historical Collections
PO Box 110571
Juneau, AK 99811-0571

Location: 333 Willoughby Avenue, 8th floor in State Office Building, Juneau.

Reference Desk:
907.465.2921

Historical Collections:
907.465.2925

General Library: asl@alaska.gov
Historical Collections: asl.historical@alaska.gov

Website: http://library.alaska.gov/forpublic.html#genealogy

Alaska US GenWeb Census Project – records from 1900-1940

Alaska US GenWeb Census Project : http://www.us-census.org/states/alaska/

Alaska Church Records

Church and synagogue records are a valuable resource, especially for baptisms, marriages, and burials that took place before 1900. There are a few challenges to locating and accessing church records, such as the multitude of religious denominations that exist. Once found however, they can reveal information about your ancestor that other records do not. You will need to at least have an idea of your ancestor's religious denomination, and in most cases you will have to visit a brick and mortar establishment to view them. Below are links archives that maintain church records, as well as a few databases that can be viewed online.

Bureau of Vital Statistics – All surviving copies of Russian Orthodox records.

Bureau of Vital Statistics : http://dhss.alaska.gov/dph/VitalStats/Pages/default.aspx

Many denominations with Alaska records have collected their data into central repositories. Following are a collection of addresses you can write to find out where their records are located.

Alaska Moravian Church
P.O. Box 545
Bethel, AK 99559
Headquarters:
Bethlehem, PA
Tel: (610) 867-7566
Fax: (610) 866-9223

Website: http://www.alaskamoravian.org/

St. Herman's Theological Seminary (Russian Orthodox)
414 Mission Road
Kodiak, AK 99615
Tel: (907) 486-3524
Fax: (907) 486-5935

Email: info@sthermanseminary.org

Website: http://www.sthermanseminary.org/

Diocese of Juneau (Roman Catholic) – includes Juneau,
Ketchikan Gateway, Sitka, Skagaway, Prince of Wales Outer
Ketchikan, Wrangell, Haines, Petersburg, and Yakutat-Angoon.
419 Sixth Street
Juneau, AK 99801
Tel: (907) 586-2227
Fax: (907) 463-3237

Website: http://www.dioceseofjuneau.org/

Diocese of Fairbanks (Roman Catholic) – includes Fairbanks,
Southeast Fairbanks, North Slope, Wade Hampton, North West
Arctic, Bethel, Fairbanks North Star, and Yukon-Koyukuk.

1316 Peger Road
Fairbanks, AK 99701
Tel: (907) 374-9500
Email: info@cbna.org

Website: http://www.cbna.info/

Archdiocese of Anchorage (Roman Catholic) – includes Aleutian Islands, Anchorage, Bristol Bay, Kodiak Island, Kenai Peninsula, Dillingham, Valdez Cordoba, and Matanuska Susitna.

225 Cordova Street
Anchorage, AK 99501
Tel: (907) 258-7898

Email: Contact via online form
Website: http://www.archdioceseofanchorage.org/

AlaskaWeb.org – records of Native Alaskans in religious archives - contains a listing of all known organizations that maintain genealogical records of interest to Native Alaskans.

AlaskaWeb.org: http://alaskaweb.org/native/aknatrecs.html

Alaska Military Records

More than 40 million Americans have participated in some time of war service since America was colonized. The chance of finding your ancestor amongst those records is exceptionally high. Military records can even reveal individuals who never actually served, such as those who registered for the two World Wars but were never called to duty.

U.S. military personnel have been in Alaska since 1867, although most of them were from the lower 48 states.

Below are a number of links to websites and archives that contain Alaska military records.

Alaska State Archives - a list of all Alaskans who served in the army, navy and marine corps during the Great War. Records include the name, age, residence, place and date of entry, branch of service, service record, and date, place and type of discharge.

Alaska State Archives:
http://archives.alaska.gov/for_researchers/for_researchers.html

U.S. National Archives – WWI Draft registration cards, casualties lists, WWI and WWII service records, Korean War records, Vietnam War records, Civil War and Spanish-American War records, and casualties lists.

U.S. National Archives :
http://www.archives.gov/research/military/veterans/online.html

LDS Family History Library - enlistment registers for the regular army, 1798 to 1914 providing name, rank, unit, occupation, commanders names, physical description, and birthplace.

LDS Family History Library:
https://familysearch.org/search/collection/1880762

US Department of Veterans Affairs Nationwide Gravesite Locator – includes information on veterans and their family members buried in veterans and military cemeteries having a government grave marker.

US Department of Veterans Affairs Nationwide Gravesite Locator: http://gravelocator.cem.va.gov/

Alaska Cemetery Records

As convenient as it is to search cemetery records online, keep in mind that there are a few disadvantages over visiting a cemetery in person. They are:

- Tombstone information may not always be accurately transcribed

- The arrangement of the graves in a cemetery can be crucial as family members are often buried next to each other or in the same grave. This arrangement is not always preserved in the alphabetical indexes that are found online.

With that information in mind, the following websites have databases that can be searched online for Alaska Cemetery records.

Find a Grave – over 100 million grave records can be searched on this site. Search can be conducted by name, location, or cemetery name.

Find a Grave: http://www.findagrave.com/

Interment.net - A free online database containing cemetery records from thousands of cemeteries around the world. Consists of approximately 4 million cemetery records.

Interment.net: http://www.interment.net/

Tombstone Transcription Project - death and burial records

Tombstone Transcription Project:

http://usgwtombstones.org/alaska/alaska.html

Municipality of Anchorage Master Burial List – burial and cemetery records

Municipality of Anchorage Master Burial List:
http://hhs.muni.org/MPCWebMap/

Alaska Cemeteries – cemetery records and tombstone inscriptions

Alaska Cemeteries:
http://www.alaskagenealogy.com/cemeteries.htm

Billion Graves – as the name implies, you can search a billion records including headstone photos, transcriptions, cemetery records, and grave locations.

Billion Graves:
http://billiongraves.com/pages/search/index.php#cemetery

Alaska Obituaries

Obituaries can reveal a wealth about our ancestor and other relatives. You can search **Alaska Newspaper Obituaries Listings** from hundreds of Alaska newspapers online for free.

Alaska Newspaper Obituaries Listings:
http://obituarieshelp.org/alaska_newspaper_obituaries.html

Alaska Dispatch News: http://www.legacy.com/obituaries/adn/

Anchorage Newspapers Obituary Index:
http://www.muni.org/Departments/library/Pages/ObitIndex.aspx

AlaskaWeb.org: http://alaskaobits.net/obituaries/

Alaska Wills and Probate Records

The documents found in a probate packet may include a complete inventory of a person's estate, newspaper entries, witness testimony, a copy of a will, list of debtors and creditors, names of executors or trustees, names of heirs. They can not only tell you about the ancestor you're currently researching, but lead to other ancestors. Most of these records must be accessed at a county court or clerk's office, but some can be found online as well.

Alaska State Archives Probate Index – index of probate files from 1883-1960.

Alaska State Archives Probate Index: http://archives.alaska.gov/pdfs/collection_guides/probate_index.pdf

Immigration and Naturalization Records

The naturalization process generated many types of records, including petitions, declarations of intention, and oaths of allegiance. District Courts of Alaska were the designated authority for overseeing the naturalization process. Evolving from a single district court in Sitka in1884, the district courts were subsequently organized into four separate divisions. Different courts maintained different naturalization records, and the best place to access naturalization records for Alaska is at the **Alaska State Archives.** They have a searchable online index that includes over 6,000 files from the courts of Petersburg, Juneau, Skagway, Nome, Wrangell, and Cordova.

Alaska State Archives: http://archives.alaska.gov/

One of the biggest challenges facing family historians is locating information about immigrant ancestors. Discovering the name of your ancestor's original town, city, county, parish, or country of origin is an important goal. Russians were the first Caucasians to inhabit Alaska, and many settlers came from the lower states during the Gold Rush. Some useful links for Alaska Immigration records are:

Alaskan Ports, 1906-1946 – index maintained by the US National Archives of Aliens arriving in Alaska ports carrying passengers from Russia, Canada, Austria, Montenegro, Italy, Great Britain, Greece, Japan, Norway, Sweden, and other European countries.

Alaskan Ports, 1906-1946:
http://www.archives.gov/research/immigration/port/alaska.html

Alaska City Directories

City directories are similar to telephone directories in that they list the residents of a particular area. The difference though is what is important to genealogists, and that is they pre-date telephone directories. You can find an ancestor's information such as their street address, place of employment, occupation, or the name of their spouse. A one-stop-shop for finding city directories in Alaska is the **Alaska Online Historical Directories** which contains a listing of every available city and historical directory related to Alaska.

Alaska Online Historical Directories: https://sites.google.com/site/onlinedirectorysite/Home/usa/ak

Alaska Railroad Records

Construction and operation of a railroad in Territory of Alaska was commissioned by the Alaska Railroad Act on March 12, 1914. Construction was overseen by the Alaska Engineering Commission to supervise construction and the railroad opened, July 15, 1923. The **US National Archives and Records Administration** holds the personnel and administration records from 1933-1968.

US National Archives and Records Administration: http://www.archives.gov/research/guide-fed-records/groups/322.html

Aleutian Islands Resources

A special page dedicated to researching ancestors from the Aleutian Islands has been constructed as part of the **Alaska GenWeb Project**. They have a multitude of Aleut-focused resources.

Alaska GenWeb Project:
http://www.rootsweb.ancestry.com/~akaleute/

Missing Matriarchs – Resources for Researching Female Alaska Ancestors

Looking for female ancestors requires an adjustment of how we view traditional records sources. A woman's identity was often under that of her husband, and often individual records for them can be difficult to locate. The following resources are effective in locating female ancestors in Alaska where traditional records may not reveal them.

Marriage and Divorce Records

- State Archives

- Library of Congress, Washington D.C. – *Index to Baptisms, Marriages and Deaths in the Archives of the Russian Orthodox Church in Alaska 1816-1866.* film 0944197

- District Court - Sitka 1884 -1903

- District Court - Eagle City, Juneau, and St. Michaels, 1903-1943

- District Court - Fairbanks, 1909-1943

- District Court - Anchorage, 1943-1959

- Anchorage Historical Commission – *Index to Births, Deaths, Marriages, and Divorces in Fairbanks Newspapers, 1903-1930.*

Native Alaskan Census Records

Miscellaneous minor census reports have been taken for various outposts, islands, and villages and are available for viewing on microfilm at the library of Congress, film 0982947. They are

- Annual Census of Pribilof Islands, 1890-1895

- Census of Sirka, 1870,1880,and 1881

- Census of Saint Paul Island, 1870,1904, and 1906

- Census of Eskimos at Cape Smythe Village, 1885

Bibliographies

- *The Alaska-Yukon Gold Book: A Roster of the Progressive Men and Women Who Were the Argonauts of the Klondike Gold Stampede* (Seattle: Sourdough Stampede Association, film 1598025)

- *Women of the Klondike*, Frances Backhouse (Whitecap Books, 1995)

- *The Entangling Net: Alaska's Commercial Fishing Women Tell Their Lives,* Leslie Leyland Fields (University of Illinois Press, 1997)

- *A Sense of History: A Reference Guide to Alaska's Women*, Roberta L. Graham (Anchorage: Alaska Women's Commission, 1985)

- *Women Who Braved the Far North: 200 Years of Alaskan Women*, Wendy H. Jones (Grossmont Press, 1976)

- *The Roles of Men and Women in Eskimo Culture,* Naomi M. Giffen (Library of Congress, film 1009060)

- *Klondike Women: True Tales of the 1897-1899 Gold Rush,* Melanie J. Mayer (Swallow Press, 1989)

- *Documenting Alaskan History: Guide to Federal Archives Relating to Alaska,* (National Archives and Records Administration)

- *Good Time Girls of the Alaska Yukon Gold Rush,* Lael Morgan (Epicenter Press, 1998)

Selected Resources for Alaska Women's History

Alaska Native Language Center

University of Alaska

ANLC Box 111

Fairbanks, AK, 99775-0120

Archives and Manuscript Dept.

University of Alaska

3211 Providence Dr. K-106

Anchorage, AK 99508

Common Alaska Surnames

The following surnames are among the most common in Alaska. The list is by no means exhaustive. If your surname doesn't appear in the list it doesn't mean that you have no Alaskan connections, only that your surname may be less common.

Addie, Agnes, Armitage, Ault, Bain, Banning, Bardsly, Barkley, Bateman, Beekman, Betty, Billingsly, Bird, Blakley, Bolin, Borden, Bozonier, Bray, Brisbane, Brisbin, Brooks, Brown, Bruner, Burke, Bush, Butler, Buzzel, Campbell, Carl, Carroll, Carswell, Cockrell, Combs, Connley, Cook, Coombes, Cornell, Cornett, Cox, Crawford, Creighton, Crumbaker, Cubitta, Cuthbertson, Dagen, Dager, Daniels, Dent, Derschau, Diamond, Dobbin, Dodd, Dodson, Donaldson, Dorchette, Duerst, Dunn, Elenor, Elizabeth, Elliot, Elliott, Engle, Erna, Esq., Everidge, Fast, Faxon, Ferrell, Finney, Flack, Force, Foreman, Frandsen, Frazier, Fugate, Fulton, Gage, Gall, Gallagher, Gardner, Garrett, Gettler, Getty, Gilchrist, Gillett, Gillis, Glasscock, Gookin, Graham, Griffits, Grigsby, Guest, Guffy, Gurtler, Hall, Hanson, Harding, Harsha, Hayden, Healey, Hensley, Hickey, Hinckley, Holland, Holmes, Hood, Hooper, Hudson, Humphry, Iacono, Imke, Jannet, Jared, Jean, Jensen, Johnson, Jones, Jr., Kangas, Kathy, Kelley, Kelly, Kennedy, Kent, Kerns, Kurkowski, Lanier, Lant, Lasseter, Laughart, Law, Ledinton, Lewis, Linn, Livingston, Livingstone, Lloyd, Lockwood, Long, Lovett, Luther, Lytle, MacDonald, MacDonough, Maguire, Mains, Mairs, Mamulski, Mapson, Marchese, Margaret, Marry, Martin, Mary, Mason, Mathis, Matthews, McAllister, McArthur, McClellan, McClelland, McCollum, McCoy, Mccoy, McCoy, McCrea, McCurdy, McDonald, McDougall, McEachron, Mceachron, McEachron, Mceachron, McEachron, Mceachron, McFaddin, McFarland, McKie, McKnight, McMillen, McMurry, McNaughton, Mcnaughton, McNaughton, Mcnaughton, McNaughton, McNeil,

McNeiley, McNish, Merrie, Meyers, Miller, Mills, Morris, Morrison, Mosley, Moyer, Murmaw, Murphy, Nance, Nancy, Nantz, Needham, Nelson, Nikolai, Ogden, Orcutt, Owens, Pace, Palakowski, Patrick, Penick, Picbull, Pickle, Polly, Pratt, Proudfit, Rachael, Randall, Recky, Reed, Reid, Richardson, Rigot, Ritchie, Roberts, Robertson, Rockwell, Rockwood, Roderick, Roe, Rowan, Rushing, Sallee, Santos, Savage, Schultig, Seitter, Sharp, Shaw, Shippee, Siemens, Sizemore, Slett, Small, Smith, Sr., Stacy, Stagg, Stapleton, Steele, Stephenson, Stevenson, Stewart, Stone, Stuart, Sutherland, Sylvester, Talbot, Taylor, Telford, Tinkey, Todd, Tompkins, Trisdale, Tull, Turner, Tutt, unknown, Unknown, VanVliet, Vine, Wade, Walker, Wallace, Walters, Ward, Warren, Watson, Wharry, White, Whitehead, Whiteman, Williams, Wilson, Witham, Worley, Wortman, Yeager, Zehner, Zeise

www.ingramcontent.com/pod-product-compliance
Lightning Source LLC
Chambersburg PA
CBHW060443290526
45793CB00002B/555

"In all of us there is a hunger, marrow-deep, to know our heritage, to know who we are and where we came from."

Author: Alex Haley

About the Author

Gary L. Morris worked from 2009 to 2014 as a professional researcher for a major player in the genealogy field. After tracing his family back to 1683, he has decided to publish these helpful guides to share the valuable information he has discovered during his career with others, to help them to trace their family lineages. An avid genealogist himself, he hopes you fill find this guide factual, thorough, helpful, and most of all, effective in helping you to find your family members.

ISBN 9781505359374

90000

9 781505 359374

PROTOCOL
AMENDING THE CONVENTION
BETWEEN
THE GOVERNMENT OF THE UNITED STATES OF AMERICA
AND
THE GOVERNMENT OF THE FRENCH REPUBLIC
FOR THE AVOIDANCE OF DOUBLE TAXATION
AND THE PREVENTION OF FISCAL EVASION
WITH RESPECT TO TAXES ON INCOME AND CAPITAL,
SIGNED AT PARIS ON AUGUST 31, 1994,
AS AMENDED BY THE PROTOCOL SIGNED ON DECEMBER 8, 2004